THE COLD WAR CHRONICLES

Sputnik and
the Space Race

Jordan Johnson

Cavendish
Square

New York

Published in 2018 by Cavendish Square Publishing, LLC
243 5th Avenue, Suite 136, New York, NY 10016

First Edition

Website: cavendishsq.com

This publication represents the opinions and views of the author based on his or her personal experience, knowledge,
and research. The information in this book serves as a general guide only. The author and publisher have used their best
efforts in preparing this book and disclaim liability rising directly or indirectly from the use and application of this book.

CPSIA Compliance Information: Batch #CS17CSQ

All websites were available and accurate when this book was sent to press.

Library of Congress Cataloging-in-Publication Data

Names: Johnson, Jordan.
Title: Sputnik and the space race / Jordan Johnson.
Description: New York : Cavendish Square Publishing, 2018. | Series: The Cold War chronicles | Includes index.
Identifiers: ISBN 9781502627322 (library bound) | ISBN 9781502627223 (ebook)
Subjects: LCSH: Space race--History--Juvenile literature. | Sputnik satellites--History--Juvenile literature. |
Astronautics--United States--History--Juvenile literature. | Astronautics--Soviet Union--History--Juvenile literature.
Classification: LCC TL793.K55 2018 | DDC 629.4/109046--dc23

Editorial Director: David McNamara
Editor: Jodyanne Benson
Copy Editor: Rebecca Rohan
Associate Art Director: Amy Greenan
Designer: Alan Sliwinski
Production Coordinator: Karol Szymczuk
Photo Research: J8 Media

Printed in the United States of America

CONTENTS

The Soviet flag and the American flag

On Your Mark, Get Set...

I t's the early 1950s. The Second World War between the Axis and Allied powers has just ended, and for a while, people can breathe a collective sigh of relief. The threat of Nazi tyranny seems to be ending, and it appears that the Allied powers have prevailed in defending their freedom. With the war over, treaties signed, and the new presence of nuclear weapons and energy for a growing number of countries, it's time to rebuild and to repair all the damage to structures and economies that war brings. Many countries go back to focusing on their own goals, using the recent war as a reason to take new actions and stances, and it's not long before more problems, like the threat of nuclear annihilation, rise from the ashes of the war. This is how the world becomes the stage for a new type of conflict just as dangerous, despite significantly fewer numbers of bombs being dropped. This is the **Cold War**, and the tension will last for nearly half a century.

History is not always neat and tidy when it comes to identifying the exact moment when a conflict starts, but most of the time, it's not too hard to find the moment when people start fighting and look back at what events, decisions, and circumstances led up to that fight. However, the years between the end of the Second World War and the early 1990s were a time in history when, rather than armies battling over strategic resources, land, or ideologies, there was only tension between groups of allies who wanted to assert dominance. During this period of tension, the United States and its allies competed for superiority with the **Union of Soviet Socialist Republics** (often simply called the **Soviet Union** or the **USSR**), which was a confederation of Russia and its other allies.

To some, it might have come as a bit of a surprise that two groups that had been allies during the Second World War could become opponents so quickly after defeating a common enemy, but that's what happened. During the war, the United States and Russia were allies, although the alliance was uneasy due to the fact that the United States was uncomfortable with the Communist ideals that Russia and many of its surrounding nations were beginning to favor. When World War II ended, and the technology for creating nuclear weapons was available to both the United States and the Soviet Union, the focus of the two superpowers shifted from fighting the threat of the Axis powers to the conflict of **Communism** versus **capitalism**. However, since both the United States and the Soviet Union possessed nuclear weapons, neither side wanted open conflict because in the

Joseph Stalin, shown here, was the leader of the Soviet Union until 1953.

case of open war between the two sides, both would be completely devastated by nuclear attacks.

Rather than open fighting, both sides rushed to find ways to assert superiority over the other in the hopes that scaring and demoralizing the other side would help persuade them not to attack. This led to rapid advances in engineering and technology with both sides starting projects that were on new frontiers of discovery and innovation. Many of these discoveries eventually led to some of the technologies we still use today. One of the most notable chapters in this age of competition was the **space** race.

On October 4, 1957, the Soviet Union launched a **satellite** named *Sputnik* (Russian for "traveling companion") that weighed 184 pounds (83.5 kilograms). The satellite took ninety-eight minutes to circle Earth while transmitting radio signals. This launch signaled the beginning of a highly competitive space race in which both sides of the Cold War devoted vast resources to advance the research and technology needed to gain superiority over the other in terms of space exploration. These challenges were used to determine which civilization was the greatest. The successes and failures of each side's space program (as well as other technological developments) were seen by the other side as representations of the strengths and weaknesses of the nation. Therefore, both sides wanted to prove that they could be the first, the best, and the bravest when it came to the exploration of outer space and the **orbit** of our own planet, and eventually, the exploration of other bodies in our solar system.

The first chapter of this book will discuss the time leading up to the space race. This will include topics such as the end of the Second World War, the formation of the **North Atlantic Treaty Organization (NATO),** the change in attitudes between the United States and the USSR, and some of the early events in the Cold War that led up to the launch of *Sputnik.*

The second chapter of this book will examine the space race itself, highlighting different moments from the perspectives of both the United States and the USSR. It will establish a timeline of events starting from the initial race to launch satellites into orbit up to the landing of **astronauts** on the moon.

Chapter three will highlight key individuals participating in the space race, including notable scientists, astronauts, and other heroes. (Some weren't even human!) This will include a look into the motivations behind the individuals discussed in the chapter as well as their direct and indirect impact on the space race and the Cold War.

Chapter four will examine some of the technologies and products, big and small, that came about as a result of the space race and the Cold War as well as discuss the political climate leading to and surrounding different events. It will show how minor problems, such as using writing instruments in space, led to innovations that helped economies grow as efforts to win the space race grew.

Chapter five will highlight the effects of the space race and the Cold War on life during and after the events that took place. It will discuss the ways that life today is still influenced by the decisions and circumstances of the efforts of the United States and the USSR.

The *Enola Gay*, the plane that carried "Little Boy," was named after the pilot's mother, Enola Gay Tibbets.

Mounting Tensions

O n Monday, August 6, 1945, the face of warfare was forever changed by the dropping of just two bombs. Carried by an American Boeing B-52 Stratofortress bomber plane, the two bombs, nicknamed Fat Man and Little Boy, were dropped over the Japanese cities of Hiroshima and Nagasaki, resulting in many deaths and massive destruction of property. These bombs, which utilized atomic technology to create an entirely new level of destruction, could outclass several tons of conventional explosives. This category of weapon would become known as weapons of mass destruction. It was clear to Japan and the rest of the world that the United States possessed military capability well beyond the forces of Japan. The Japanese surrender came soon after, signaling the end of the Second World War on the Pacific front only a few months after the war had ended on the European front the previous spring.

With the war over, the unsteady alliance between the United States and the Soviet Union also came to an end, and relations between the rival world superpowers quickly grew tense. What caused the tension? The United States was a capitalist nation, which meant that businesses were owned privately and run for profit, whereas the Soviet Union favored Communism, a political ideology that dictated that all property and businesses be owned by the government rather than private citizens. Both nations needed expansion for their ideals to work, and the clash between two civilizations and cultures resulted in severe tensions that would last until the early 1990s. This period in history is known as the Cold War.

The Potsdam Conference

As previously agreed, after the surrender of Germany in May 1945, United States president Harry Truman, British prime minister Winston Churchill, and Soviet leader Joseph Stalin met in Potsdam, Germany to discuss what would happen now that the war in Europe was at an end. This discussion, called the Potsdam Conference, aimed to set reconstruction in motion for the countries affected by the war and to determine where any post-war border lines needed to be drawn or redrawn. One of the most important points of the conference was to decide what should be done with Germany, one of the major aggressors of the war.

Because of the heavy toll the German invasion had taken on his nation and its people, Stalin wanted to force Germany to make heavy reparations in the form of money paid to the Allied nations, with half of the money going to the Soviet Union. This concerned Truman and the other leaders because a similar policy had been enacted against Germany following the First World War, and many considered it to have been one of the sources of unrest and destabilization in Germany that led to the rise of Nazi power and the Second World War. Instead, in order to break the cycle and avoid repeating history, President Truman proposed a less severe option. According to the US Department of State's historical website, "Truman and his Secretary of State, James Byrnes, were determined to mitigate the treatment of Germany by allowing the occupying nations to exact reparations only from

World leaders at the Potsdam Conference discuss the future of post-war Germany.

their own zone of occupation." This meant splitting Germany into sections, with each section paying reparations to either the United States, Britain, France, or the Soviet Union. Not only would this curb the amount of reparations due from Germany overall, but it would also reduce the portion of the reparations that would go to the USSR. However, the German capital of Berlin was nestled firmly within the area that was to be given to the Soviet Union. To prevent giving the USSR too much influence in the capital, the city itself was also divided between the United States, British, French, and Russian negotiators.

The next major decision made during the Potsdam Conference was a systematic dismantling of all the systems and industries created by the Nazi Party, including the repeal of authoritarian and discriminatory policies and the demilitarization of German industry. Demilitarization of industry required the dismantling of any manufacturing equipment that could be put to military use as well as the dissolution or elimination of any military or paramilitary organizations that remained after the German surrender. The way would soon be paved for democratically elected leaders to help reconstruct the German government, and an organization called the Allied Control Commission (with representatives from Britain, France, the United States, and the Soviet Union) would help run things in the meantime.

Problems at Potsdam

The Potsdam Conference wasn't without its problems, however. One of the largest issues that came up involved the redrawing of borders of German, Polish, and USSR territories. Poland, Hungary, and Czechoslovakia were all given a section of German land, but this meant that the Germans who lived there were being evicted and deported from land that had once been their home. A mass exodus of this type could send a wave of unhappy citizens into what was left of Germany and make the reconstruction effort problematic. Although no official resolutions on the subject were passed, the United States and Britain both made statements insisting that any necessary deportations should be carried out as humanely as possible and asked that Poland, Czechoslovakia, and Hungary temporarily stop deporting people to ease the transition over time.

Another major point of tension at the conference was the fact that President Truman believed that the United States's possession of the world's only nuclear weapons at the time would give him more sway over negotiations, allowing him to hold firm to his points against the demanding and diplomatically aggressive Soviet Union. In fact, many historians agree that the decision to use atomic weapons on Japan in 1945 was also meant in part to intimidate the Soviet Union. It wouldn't be long, however, before the Soviet Union would have its own nuclear arsenal. Toward the end of World War II, several of the scientists and other personnel working on atomic projects had secretly given information on nuclear weapons to the Soviet Union, creating the start of an arms race between the United States and Soviet Union that would last throughout most of the Cold War.

Berlin Divided

After the negotiations at the Potsdam Conference reached a conclusion, it seemed as if the world was on the right track toward reconstruction and post-war recovery. However, over the course of two years, a Communist government was established in two countries. First, Albania succeeded in establishing a major Communist movement in January 1947, followed by Communists seizing power in Poland just one year later. This prompted a response from President Truman the following March. According to History.com, "In a dramatic speech to a joint session of Congress, President Harry S. Truman asks for US assistance for Greece and Turkey to forestall communist domination of the two nations. Historians have often cited Truman's address, which came to be known as the Truman Doctrine, as the official declaration of the Cold War." Truman felt it was up to the United States to stand up to Communism wherever the threat of its expansion was occurring.

In 1948, the USSR blocked off all railways, roads, and waterways into and out of Berlin, attempting to prevent the purchase of goods by people in the districts controlled by the United States, Britain, and France. This is considered one of the opening moves of the Cold War, and the response of the Americans, British, and French was to circumvent the blocked roads and railways by using aircraft to deliver supplies in what became known as the **Berlin Airlift**. This effort lasted for about a year with almost two and a half million tons delivered to the people stuck behind the blockade. Although the blockade eventually ceased, this

This cargo plane is carrying supplies during one of the nearly one hundred trips Allied planes made per day.

Toys that Won the Cold War

A major part of the tension between the United States and the Soviet Union was the rivalry between capitalism and communism. These ideologies influenced and shaped the political and economic dimensions of the country. One of the major tactics of the United States was to show how prosperous it was through a golden age of toys and games available to children because the country was doing so well due to its free markets and consumerism.

Many of these toys and games, made popular during the 1940s and early 1950s, are still available and popular today. These toys include Silly Putty, which was originally created by accident in an attempt to create a new kind of rubber for tank treads. The toy became a hit due to its relatively inexpensive production costs combined with its novel properties. Another example of notable toys from the Cold War era includes games like jacks and tiddly-winks; board games like Candy Land, checkers, Clue, and Parcheesi; and many types of rideable toys such as tricycles, pedal-cars, and the famous steel Radio Flyer wagon, which cost nine dollars in 1949. That amount would be over ninety dollars today, but the toy's popularity and longevity would make it, alongside Silly Putty, one of the toys that helped win the Cold War.

Other popular items included play sets for different professions such as doctors or police officers, typewriters, musical instruments, Barbie dolls, toy soldiers, chemistry sets, cooking sets, model planes and other vehicles, and other items that the American economy could afford to produce as toys for children.

blockade tactic would eventually become the building of the **Berlin Wall**, which would later create a deeper divide between East Berlin and West Berlin that would remain in place until the 1980s.

The Foundation of NATO

In response to the growing presence of Communism and the Soviet attempt to force Western control out of Berlin, the United States and several other nations agreed to form a cooperative effort called the North Atlantic Treaty Organization (NATO) in the spring of 1949, agreeing to defend each other and help resist Communist expansion. This started a long tradition of military cooperation between the United States and its NATO allies.

The following summer, after obtaining the plans and instructions using espionage, the Soviet Union detonated its own atomic bomb, proving its own nuclear capability to the world and signaling the start of a prolonged arms race between itself and the United States. With the knowledge that Communist influence was not only spreading but strengthening, many suspected that the domino theory, which stated that if one nation became Communist that others nearby would follow, was a very real possibility. It wasn't long before both the United States and the Soviet Union would gather enough nuclear weapons not only to destroy each other, but also to be a risk to the entire human race in the event of a nuclear war. Eventually, the United States and the Soviet Union would agree on a strategy called **mutually assured destruction (MAD)**. This strategy came from the fact that nuclear **missiles** take enough time to travel from one nation to the other that the defender would have enough time to launch every weapon it had against the attacker, assuring that both sides would be obliterated no matter who attacked first.

The Korean War

In June 1950, war broke out in Korea when several thousand troops from the Communist-led Democratic People's Republic of Korea in the north marched across the 38th parallel into territory owned by the Republic of Korea to the south, which favored Western capitalism. With this invasion being the first major fight against Communist-led forces, the United States gave aid to the South Korean forces, believing now was the time to act whereas before there were only declarations. According to History.com, "This invasion was the first military action of the Cold War. By July, American troops had entered the war on South Korea's behalf. As far as American officials were concerned, it was a war against the forces of international communism itself."

Much of the reasoning behind the United States taking part in the Korean War was due to the growing support for the domino theory that suggested if one nation in Asia fell to Communism, others would follow in a chain reaction. This same domino theory would be much of the justification for the Vietnam War later. Although the fighting was fierce, resulting in some five million casualties (both military and civilian), the peninsula of Korea remains divided between the communist north and the capitalist south today.

The Korean War ended in 1953 with the creation of an armistice, giving South Korea fifteen hundred square miles of territory and creating a two-mile-wide (3.2 kilometers) demilitarized zone (DMZ) that is still the dividing line between North and South Korea to this day.

While Communists were seizing power in Asia, the United States was attempting to find its own ways to gather allies and influence other nations to join its side during the Cold War. In 1953, just after the end of the Korean War, Iran overthrew its government in a coup, assisted by the United States in the form of resources and financial support. In place of former leader Mohammed Mosaddeq, the Shah of Iran was put into power and would serve as an ally to the United States until the late 1970s. Just a year after the coup in Iran, another coup assisted by the United States overthrew the government of Guatemala. September of that same year saw the formation of the **Southeast Asia Treaty Organization (SEATO)**, a partner to NATO, which was also dedicated to fighting Communism and defending against its expansion.

In response to the formations of both NATO and SEATO, the USSR and its allies, Albania, Bulgaria, East Germany, Hungary, Poland, Romania, and Czechoslovakia, formed a similar alliance called the Warsaw Pact. The creation of the Warsaw Pact seemed to indicate that the world was poised and ready to start a third world war. With both sides gathering more and more nuclear weapons and organizing themselves into alliances sworn to protect one another from any enemies, history appeared to be on the brink of repeating itself in a new and terribly destructive way.

The Geneva Summit

In July 1955, with the world still on the brink of nuclear war and the potential annihilation of the human race, another meeting was held between world leaders. But rather than discussing post-war reconstruction efforts, the goal of this meeting, held in Geneva, Switzerland (historically neutral), was to attempt to bring an end to the Cold War, or at least make some of the first steps in untangling the tense web that threatened to entangle the entire world in a nuclear apocalypse. This summit meeting included attendance from United States president Dwight D. Eisenhower, British prime minister Anthony Eden, French premier Edgar Faure, and Nikolai Bulganin from the USSR. One of the biggest concerns during the Geneva Summit was the ongoing arms race between the United States and the USSR. In an attempt to lower tensions between the two nations that could lead to nuclear war, Eisenhower proposed an agreement to exchange maps of the locations of both sides' nuclear weapons installations. Then, each side would be allowed to conduct surveillance flights over the other nation to verify the location of nuclear weapons. This proposal was known as the "open skies" proposal and was seen by many as a gesture of good faith toward the Soviet Union.

The Soviet Union's reaction to Eisenhower's proposal was not favorable, with Communist leader Nikita Khrushchev quoted as saying the plan was an "espionage plot." The rejection of the proposal was something Eisenhower expected, however, and he was later quoted as intentionally proposing a plan the Soviet Union would reject. According

World leaders at the Geneva Summit attempt to de-escalate tensions.

Edgar Faure: Resistance Fighter, Politician, Novelist

When studying the Cold War, it's easy to miss the opportunity to learn about some very interesting people who were present for important parts of it, but were otherwise not always front-and-center in terms of what many people remember. Edgar Faure, who was present at the Geneva Summit, was a very interesting person. Born on August 18, 1908, as the son of a military medic, Edgar Faure took part in the French Resistance during the Second World War.

In 1931, he married Lucie Meyer, who was the daughter of a silk merchant. They spent their honeymoon in the Soviet Union. He served as mayor of Port-Lesney in 1947 and held the position for twenty-four years. He held positions for various ministries in French government including the ministries of budget, justice, finance, and agriculture. He served as president of the National Assembly for a short time in 1952, and for a full year in 1955. He saw the rise in power of Charles de Gaulle, who became the 18th president of France.

During de Gaulle's time as president, Faure was selected as de Gaulle's choice to handle various delicate diplomatic missions all over the world. In 1966, he was appointed as Minister of Agriculture, and in 1968, he became Minister of Education. He was also credited with great reforms that revitalized the French university system. After de Gaulle resigned from the presidency, Faure continued to serve the French government in various positions, including the National Assembly and European Parliament. Alongside his political and academic achievements, he wrote several essays, mystery novels and memoirs, using the pseudonym Edgar Sanday. He died on March 30, 1988.

to History.com, "[Eisenhower] knew the Soviets would never accept the plan, but thought that their rejection of the idea would make the Russians look like they were the major impediment to an arms control agreement. For the Soviets, the idea of US planes conducting surveillance of their military bases was unthinkable." Part of the reason for this resistance was that the Soviet Union did not want the United States to know it had fallen far behind in the arms race. Although there was not much in terms of major decisions that came about as a result of the Geneva Summit, it was an important step in creating diplomatic relations with the Soviet Union in an attempt to ease Cold War tensions.

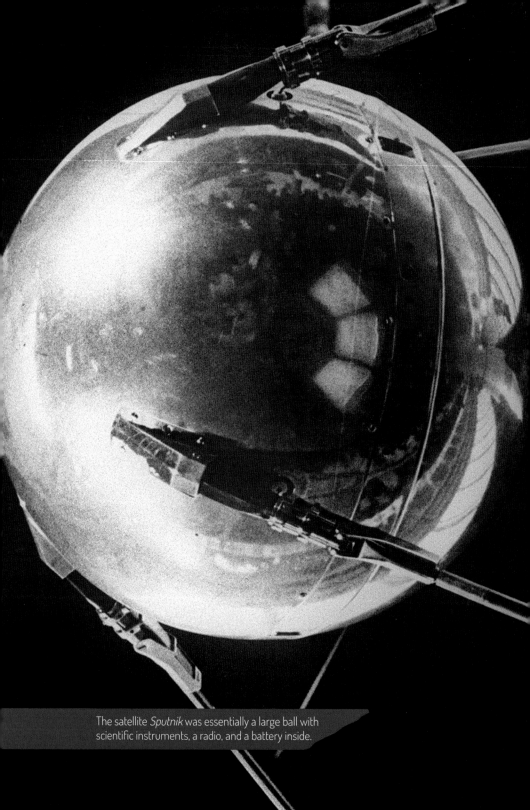

The satellite *Sputnik* was essentially a large ball with scientific instruments, a radio, and a battery inside.

CHAPTER TWO

The
Space Race

The year was 1957, and the Cold War was still a daily concern for people in the United States and the Soviet Union. Although the summit held by world leaders on both sides of the Cold War was a step forward in terms of progress toward peace, it was a small step, one overshadowed by the crushing defeat of the Hungarian Revolution by the forces of the Red Army the previous year. Tensions between NATO and the Warsaw Pact were still high, and it was unclear what the next chapter of the Cold War would hold. Little did the world know that the newest chapter was about to begin, and with it would come an age of discovery.

Sputnik: The Starter Pistol of the Space Race

On October 4, 1957, at around 10:30 p.m. Moscow time, the Soviet Union successfully launched the world's first artificial satellite into orbit. Delivered into space using the same **rocket** technology as a nuclear missile, the satellite *Sputnik* was roughly the size of a beach ball at twenty-two inches (0.56 meter) in diameter. Tasked with gathering information about Earth's upper atmosphere, *Sputnik* orbited around Earth every hour and thirty-six minutes at an incredible velocity of eighteen thousand miles (28,968 kilometers) per hour. Moving at more than twenty times the speed of sound, *Sputnik* could be seen in the morning before sunrise or the evening just after sunset with the aid of simple binoculars. Equipped with radio transmitters, *Sputnik* broadcasted signals back to Earth that could be picked up by anyone with the equipment to do so, including many amateur radio enthusiasts.

The next morning, American news companies reported on the launch, with *Sputnik* making the front page of the *New York Times*. Overall, the reaction to the launch of *Sputnik* by the American people was one of concern or even fear. After all, the threat of Communist military action was a constant occurrence in daily life through the news, and with the news of Russia being able to launch a device into orbit came the fear that Russia could have rocket technology strong enough to harm the United States. Many did not believe the Soviet Union capable of such an achievement and were surprised by the successful launch. According to History.com, "The US government, military, and scientific community were caught off guard by the Soviet technological achievement, and their united efforts to catch up with the Soviets heralded the beginning of the 'space race.'" The presence of a Soviet space program was a challenge that the United States could not ignore, and thus, the effort to compete with Russia to prove who was superior was in full swing.

Sputnik 2 and the First Astronaut

With the space race on and both sides of the Cold War rushing to assert dominance in spaceflight technology, the Soviet Union quickly organized a second launch, aiming to claim as many first moments in aerospace technology development as possible. The plan was to go beyond the first artificial satellite that they had achieved a month prior. This time, they would claim the title of the first astronaut to orbit Earth.

On November 3, 1957, the world's first astronaut to orbit Earth woke up, ate a healthy breakfast, bathed, and was led to the rocket that would carry out the mission. She was strapped securely into place and received a scratch behind the ears. Having grown up as a stray on the streets of Moscow, Laika and the other dogs in the Soviet Union's space program were selected for their hardiness and tolerance for cold temperatures. Although other dogs had taken part in sub-orbital flights, Laika had become a favorite of many of the scientists and staff.

Laika's vessel was equipped with various equipment to protect and monitor her health during her launch and orbit. She was held in place by safety straps that would protect her from the intense g-forces of the launch as well as insulated by an egg-shaped pod equipped with food and water dispensers as well as oxygen for her to breathe. She was also hooked up to machinery that could monitor her heartbeat and breathing.

Laika in a training version of the capsule that would carry her on her flight

She even had a microphone that could detect her barking, broadcasting information via radio to those controlling the mission. Although she had earned the affection of many of those involved with the mission, the effects of spaceflight on living organisms was not yet certain, and the technology for spacecraft recovery was not yet developed. Laika's flight would be the first, and her last.

At 5:30 in the evening, the launch of the *Sputnik 2* rocket carried Laika into the sky, accelerating to almost five miles (8 km) per second, carrying her toward her mission. The initial plan was that Laika would have enough oxygen for ten days, with initial reports claiming that the last of her food or a secondary tank of gas would euthanize her painlessly, but this was not the case. Although the official reports claimed she was euthanized painlessly to prevent undue suffering, it wasn't revealed for almost fifty years that due to a malfunction in the temperature regulator on the satellite, Laika passed away on the second day of her orbit around Earth due to overheating. *Sputnik 2* orbited Earth for 162 days.

The American Response: *Explorer 1* and *Explorer 2*

In January of 1958, just a few months after the launch of *Sputnik 2*, the United States launched its very own artificial satellite, known as *Explorer 1*. According to the **National Aeronautics and Space Administration (NASA)**, "Following the launch of the Soviet Union's *Sputnik 1* on October 4, 1957, the US Army Ballistic Missile Agency was directed to launch a satellite using its Jupiter C rocket developed under the direction of Dr. Wernher von Braun. The Jet Propulsion Laboratory received the assignment to design, build, and operate the artificial satellite that would serve as the rocket's payload. JPL completed this job in less than three months." The *Explorer 1* satellite discovered the Van Allen Radiation belt, which was named after the scientists who designed the instrument that could detect the cosmic rays present in orbit. It orbited Earth until it burned up upon reentry into Earth's atmosphere in 1970.

Reactions to Laika's Flight

News of the launch of *Sputnik 2*, including information about its precious cargo, prompted reactions from Americans. These reactions included mockery at the hubris of Russian scientists to pity for her plight. According to *Time* magazine, "The *Chicago American* noted: 'The Russian sputpup isn't the first dog in the sky. That honor belongs to the dog star. But we're getting too Sirius,' the piece adds. Other headline-writers treated Laika with more compassion ... The Brits were especially full of feeling for the dog—and outrage toward the Russians. 'THE DOG WILL DIE, WE CAN'T SAVE IT', wailed London's mass-minded Daily Mirror.'" Scientists who worked on the launch were later quoted as regretting the launch, claiming that the information they gained from the launch was not enough to justify sacrificing her life. The story of the legendary space dog prompted a new animal rights movement, even before the details of how she died became public.

In 1964, a monument erected in Moscow to commemorate the "Conquerors of Space" included a depiction of Laika and another monument dedicated solely to her was erected in 2008. Laika has become a symbol for animal rights as well as sacrifice for the greater good. The lesson learned from her passing strengthened resolve in terms of making spaceflight safer for all animal and human astronauts. Although her tale is one of tragedy and surrounded by a cover-up and propaganda, her sacrifice will never be forgotten by those who dare to venture among the stars that she was the first to travel.

Just three months after the successful launch of *Explorer 1*, there was a second mission to launch an artificial satellite. This mission, called Explorer 2, failed when one of the stages of the rocket failed to ignite, preventing it from reaching orbit. These missions were then handed from the Jet Propulsion Laboratory to the Goddard Spaceflight program, focusing on other missions. Luckily, just twelve days later, the successful launch of the *Vanguard 1* satellite indicated that progress was being made.

Sputnik 3

On May 15, 1958, the Soviet Union launched *Sputnik 3*, another artificial satellite with no passengers. It was designed to gather information on the composition of the upper atmosphere. According to NASA, "*Sputnik 3* was an automatic scientific laboratory spacecraft. The scientific instrumentation (twelve instruments) provided data on pressure and composition of the upper atmosphere, concentration of charged particles, photons in cosmic rays, heavy nuclei in cosmic rays, magnetic and electrostatic fields, and meteoric particles." *Sputnik 3* was the largest satellite that had been successfully launched into orbit at that point in history, and it would orbit Earth for about two years.

NASA

On the first of October, 1958, NASA was formed, replacing the National Advisory Committee on Aeronautics (NACA) with the passing of the Space Act. Among its eight official objectives were the expansion of knowledge about the upper atmosphere and space, developing safer and more effective space vehicles. Another objective was "cooperation by the United States with other nations and groups of nations in work done pursuant to this Act and in the peaceful application of the results thereof," according to NASA. Rather than being formed from previous organizations like the NACA or the Army or Air Force, NASA's creation was to be a step forward toward progress and peaceful discovery. Although the space race was formed in part due to the tensions of the Cold War, the objectives of NASA were peaceful and not intended to intimidate the USSR. Only eleven days into its mission, NASA launched the *Pioneer 1* satellite. Although it did not achieve its mission of escaping Earth's gravitational field and reaching the moon, it did travel an impressive 70,700 miles (113,780 km) and provided nearly two days' worth of data.

The Luna Missions

In January of 1959, the Soviet Union began a series of launches that aimed at collecting further information on the temperature and gas compositions in outer space. The first satellite, *Luna 1*, was launched on January 2, 1959, and was intended to impact the moon. However, it only passed within 3,728 miles (6000 km) of the moon. This was much closer than the Americans would get with the launch of *Pioneer 4* two months later. During its flight, *Luna 1* released a kilogram of sodium gas, enough to create a glowing cloud that was visible from Earth. This provided some of the first information about how gasses behaved in space. *Luna 1* wound up orbiting the sun, passing between Earth and Mars.

Luna 2 was launched in September 1959, and unlike its predecessor, managed to reach the moon, impacting its surface on the second day of its flight, causing its transmissions to stop abruptly. It carried a variety of instruments such as Geiger counters to measure radiation, but it had no means of propelling itself. Like *Luna 1*, the satellite released a cloud of sodium to aid in tracking it.

The mission of *Luna 3* just a month later was different from *Luna 1* or *Luna 2*. Rather than aiming to merely orbit or impact the surface of the moon, the satellite was equipped with solar power cells to provide electricity to a camera and small photograph processing unit. It was able to use these tools to photograph a majority of the surface of the moon and broadcast those photos back to Earth. The photos gathered by *Luna 3* of the moon's surface would be the closest photos that either side would gain until the American *Ranger 7* satellite would take close-range images five years later.

Kennedy: "We Choose to Go to the Moon."

In April 1960, the United States successfully launched *TIROS 1*, a satellite designed to test the possibility of using satellites to study Earth itself rather than merely measure radiation and temperature in orbit. *TIROS 1*, which stood for the Television Infrared Observation Satellite, was the first satellite used to observe weather on Earth's surface, with

President Kennedy's famous speech at Rice University helped motivate the nation to win the space race.

the ability to help track major storms and other important weather patterns.

The following August saw the launch of *Discoverer XIV*, a spy satellite capable of taking photographs of Earth's surface. Rather than broadcasting the photographs back to Earth via radio, where anyone with the right equipment might be able to intercept and decode the signal, the satellite was launched into orbit and then recovered by a specially equipped plane capable of snagging the satellite and reeling it in for safe recovery of its contents. Just a few months later, John F. Kennedy was elected as the thirty-fifth president of the United States.

Although the United States was not able to claim the triumph of the first man to orbit Earth, which was achieved by Russia's Yuri Gagarin in April 1961, the United States was able to get a man into space safely the following month. Alan B. Shepard, aboard the *Freedom 7* capsule, flew more than a hundred miles high and returned safely after a flight time of just over fifteen minutes. Gagarin's flight time, however, was 89 minutes. Still, with the success of Shepard's mission in mind, President Kennedy challenged the nation to keep working on the space program. According to NASA, "The popular media went wild over America's achievement and its new astronaut hero. Building on the excitement, Kennedy's famous message to Congress on May 25, 1961, set the goal 'before this decade is out, of landing a man on the Moon and returning him safely to Earth.'"

America Resolves to Reach the Moon

Following the success of Shepard's mission, the motivation for Americans to go to space was renewed despite the fact that the Russian space program seemed determined to make as many monumental achievements as possible. Although yet another successful mission conducted by the Russians put Gherman Titov into space for just over twenty-four hours, the United States was not discouraged. America had a goal and would do all that it could to reach the moon.

The first step toward the ability to land on the moon was the announcement of the Gemini program. Headed by NASA, the program set out to train and assess astronauts to determine the maximum amount of time they could travel safely in space as well as research and develop the technologies to allow them to return to Earth safely. America was determined to reach the moon, but safety was of utmost concern if the goal was to be reached with any sort of pride for the nation.

1962

In February 1962, John Glenn orbited Earth three times aboard the capsule dubbed *Friendship 7*. Although his flight was a symbolic step forward for the American spaceflight program, his flight was no simple task. A malfunction partway through the flight made it necessary to take manual control of the capsule, flying himself for the rest of his mission. After orbiting for nearly five hours, his capsule splashed into the Atlantic Ocean where he was safely recovered, instantly becoming an American hero.

Astronaut John Glenn in his space suit

According to NASA, "President John Kennedy awarded him the Space Congressional Medal of Honor. Schools and streets across the country were named after him. And a ticker tape parade in New York City celebrated his mission." Just a few months later, Glenn's mission was repeated by Scott Carpenter aboard his capsule *Aurora 7* with similar success.

On September 12, 1962, following the successes of Glenn's and Carpenter's missions, President John F. Kennedy gave a speech at William Marsh Rice University in Houston, Texas, reaffirming America's intent to go to the moon. In his speech, President Kennedy asks,

> *But why, some say, the Moon? Why choose this as our goal? And they may well ask, why climb the highest mountain? Why, 35 years ago, fly the Atlantic? Why does Rice play Texas? We choose to go to the Moon in this decade and do the other things, not because they are easy, but because they are hard; because that goal will serve to organize and measure the best of our energies and skills, because that challenge is one that we are willing to accept, one we are unwilling to postpone, and one we intend to win.*

There were two more important space race milestones on the American side in 1962. The first was a mission that carried Walter Schirra into orbit around Earth, where he orbited six times, beating Glenn's and Carpenter's flight times. The second was the Mariner 2 mission, which was the first spacecraft to pass by another planet. The capability of long-distance flight control was important for NASA to have, as it greatly improved the range at which the different parts of the solar system could be explored.

1963

Less eventful compared to other years, 1963 held only two missions. In May, L. Gordon Cooper's mission, in which he spent thirty-four hours in space, was the last American mission where a person was alone in space. In June, Valentina Tereshkova became the first woman in space, claiming another achievement for the Russian **cosmonauts**.

On November 22, 1963, President John F. Kennedy was shot and killed by Lee Harvey Oswald in Dallas, Texas. The nation mourned his passing as he was not only a popular president, but a major advocate of NASA's mission to the moon. Vice President Lyndon Baines Johnson was sworn into office shortly thereafter.

1964

In July, 1964, the Ranger 7 mission launched. Its task was to take high-resolution images of the moon's surface before impact, and the mission was a success. As the satellite was approaching the moon's surface, it transmitted more than four thousand images over the course of fifteen minutes, nearly five images per second. Gaining these images was a big step forward toward the goal of reaching the moon.

1965

In May 1965, the first **spacewalk** was performed by Russian cosmonaut Alexei Leonov, who spent twelve minutes outside his space craft. This established not only the possibility for humans to explore space in person, but the possibility for Russia to explore the moon before the United States if they reached it first. Just five days later, the launch of the first manned Gemini flight carried Lieutenant Colonel Virgil

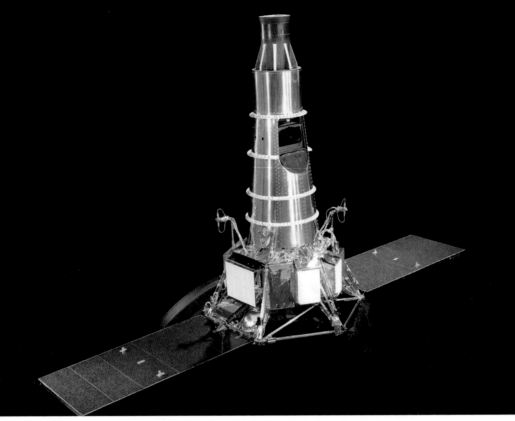

The satellite *Ranger 7* carried several cameras intended to capture images of the moon.

Ivan "Gus" Grissom and John W. Young around Earth three times. These two-person missions would pave the way toward reaching the moon. According to NASA, "NASA's two-man Gemini spaceflights demonstrated that astronauts could change their capsule's orbit, remain in space for at least two weeks, and work outside their spacecraft. They also pioneered rendezvous and docking with other spacecraft. All were essential skills to land on the moon and return safely to Earth." Grissom's part in this mission also earned him the title of the first man to travel to space twice.

The following June, Ed White performed America's first spacewalk while his flight partner Jim McDivitt remained in the capsule. Just one month later, the *Mariner 4* satellite transmitted close-range photographs of the surface of Mars. The Russian space program launched *Venus 3* in November, which became the first man-made object to impact Venus in March of 1966. Just one month after the launch of *Venus 3*, American astronauts Frank Mowman and James Lovell started a two-week long orbit on the *Gemini 7*, which managed to make the world's first spacecraft rendezvous with *Gemini 6*, crewed by Walter Schirra and Thomas Stafford.

1966

With the Luna program still underway, the Russian space program launched two more satellites, both of which achieved new milestones. First, *Luna 9* was the first satellite to make a soft landing on the moon's surface. Then, *Luna 10* became the first satellite to orbit the moon, rather than merely pass by or impact it. Two American missions duplicated the same feats, however, with *Surveyor 1* making a soft landing in June and the satellite *Lunar Orbiter 1* in August. *Lunar Orbiter 1* not only established a lunar orbit but also took a photo of Earth from the farthest distance yet. Finally, the last flight of the Gemini program, *Gemini 12*, carried astronauts James Lovell and Edwin "Buzz" Aldrin.

1967

Both sides of the space race encountered tragic accidents that highlighted the dangers of space travel in 1967. In January, Roger Chaffee, Gus Grissom, and Ed White died when a fire occurred in the capsule of *Apollo 1* during a test on the launch pad. The Russian space program lost cosmonaut Vladimir Comarov when the parachute of his capsule failed to open correctly on his return to Earth. Although these deaths rocked both sides, prompting further research into safety measures, the Russians still had success with their counterpart to the Mariner 2 mission that flew past Venus in the form of the *Venera 4* satellite, which gathered and transmitted information about the atmosphere of Venus, rather than impacting its surface.

1968

Although the first major launch of 1968 didn't occur until mid-September, the Russian space program launched the *Zond 5*, the first satellite that carried animals to return to Earth safely. It carried two turtles as well as some worms and insects. Its flight lasted six days. The next major launch, *Apollo 8*, came on December 21, carrying American astronauts Frank Worman, James Lovell, and William Anders on the first journey to the moon. On Christmas Eve, the astronauts took turns reading the book of Genesis from the bible on a radio broadcast that anyone with a radio could tune in to listen to.

1969

In January 1969, the Russian space program performed the first spacecraft docking on the Soviet side of the space race. Six months later, NASA and the United States saw the culmination of their decade-long journey toward landing on

The flag placed by American astronauts on the moon was held up by a rod across the top because there is no wind on the moon.

the moon when Neil Armstrong and Buzz Aldrin became the first two men to walk on the moon while Michael Collins orbited above them. Before setting foot on the surface of the moon, Armstrong transmitted over the radio, "That's one small step for man, one giant leap for mankind."

Cultural Impact

The success of the Apollo 11 mission marked a moment in history when humans had, for the first time, looked upon Earth in its entirety. Even before astronaut boots were imprinted upon moon dust, the crew of *Apollo 8* took a picture of Earth, small and blue, rising over the horizon of the moon's surface. The picture became iconic

This famous photograph titled "Earthrise" helped people realize that Earth was more than a mix of separate nations—it was one unified planet.

very quickly, promoting a new perspective on global events. The surface of Earth, seen by the naked eye, was not like most of the maps that were used to divide up the surface into nations. It was a whole world, a single flash of sapphire in a seemingly endless sea of the dark. As Jim Lovell put it, "The vast loneliness is awe-inspiring, and it makes you realize just what you have back there on Earth."

That image, that thought, and that feeling stuck with people, inspiring them to think on more of a global scale, rather than a national scale. Nations were inspired to strive for the technology of the future because the last decade and a half reminded them that the future could be very, very finite unless people changed it. Soon after, the United States and the rest of the world saw the rise of massive environmental and humanitarian movements, inspired by the recognition that Earth might be all that humanity has, or might ever have, for the foreseeable future. The celebration of Earth Day, Doctors Without Borders, and the Environmental Protection Agency were all founded shortly after the rise in global awareness. This would even affect the Cold War, as only a few years after Apollo 11, a joint launch between the United States and Soviet Union allowed astronauts from both sides to connect spacecraft to each other in orbit and greet each other as friends, colleagues, and fellow adventurers in the space race.

Astronaut Alan Shepard's reflective spacesuit was designed to look futuristic and protect him in flight.

CHAPTER THREE

The Faces of the Cold War

In 1961, America seemed to be losing the space race against the Soviet Union. With several successful launches completed by the Soviet space program, it seemed like NASA would never catch up to Russia's cosmonauts. The scientists and astronauts at NASA were not deterred, however. With the recent election of President John F. Kennedy, an outspoken advocate for the importance of space research, there was still hope that slow and steady progress would in fact win the race.

Alan B. Shepard

On May 5, 1961, America saw concrete proof of results of its efforts, as a rocket carried astronaut Alan B. Shepard into space. His mission took only a short while, but it was enough to make history. Although he was not the first man to ever get there, he was still an American hero, a symbol of the courage and pioneering spirit that the United States and NASA had tried to reach through the space program.

Born in East Derry, New Hampshire, on November 18, 1923, Alan Shepard grew up in New Hampshire and attended school like anyone else. After high school, he earned a bachelor of science in 1944 from the US Naval Academy, and then he graduated from the Navy Test Pilot School just seven years later. Over the course of his time as a test pilot, he accumulated eight thousand hours of flight time, almost half of which were in jet aircraft. In 1961, he became the first American man in space, and over the course of his career at NASA, he participated in several missions as the CapCom officer, in charge of communicating directly with the astronauts conducting their own missions. Later, he served as Chief of the Astronaut Office in 1963. He was awarded the Congressional Medal of Honor for Space, as well as several other awards and honorary degrees from prestigious universities all over the United States. He logged a total of 216 hours in space over the course of his life, nine hours of which were on spacewalks outside his craft. A polite, intelligent, and friendly person, in his last interview, conducted in February 1998 with CSPAN-3, he described his first time gathering with his team as one of the happiest days of his life. He passed away in July 1998 from leukemia, and he will always be remembered as an American hero.

Buzz Aldrin

Born on January 20, 1930, Edwin Eugene "Buzz" Aldrin came from a military family. His father was a colonel in the United States Air Force, and his mother was the daughter of a US Army chaplain. It's little surprise then that after he

Astronaut Buzz Aldrin secures the glove of his suit.

graduated from high school in Montclair, New Jersey, he earned a bachelor of science degree from the US Military Academy in 1951 and joined the Air Force the following year. He participated in the Korean War, flying more than sixty combat missions. After the war, he returned to schooling, and in 1962, he received a doctorate of science from the Massachusetts Institute of Technology. In 1963, he joined NASA and served as the CapCom officer for Gemini missions.

Although his first flight as an astronaut was for the Gemini 12 mission in 1966, he is best known for the Apollo 11 mission three years later, when he became the second person to walk on the moon in 1969. After the success of the Apollo 11 mission, he returned to serve in the Air Force as commander of the test pilot program until he retired in 1972. Still, his contributions to NASA and space exploration were not complete. Despite battling depression and alcoholism, he patented his designs for a spacecraft system that opened the possibility for taking humans to Mars. It was called the Aldrin Mars Cycler. He also holds three patents for his designs for a modular space station, elements of which are implemented in the International Space Station today. Aldrin is still a fierce advocate of space research and exploration, and he has written several nonfiction books (and at least one science fiction novel) inspired by his efforts as part of the space program. He also founded a non-profit organization, ShareSpace Foundation, which aims to advance education about space.

Dwight D. Eisenhower

Moments in American history are often associated with the leaders of the time. The story of United States president Dwight D. Eisenhower and his contributions to the early days of the Cold War set the stage for the space race, setting in motion a chain of events that would eventually put men on the moon, long after his term in office ended.

The thirty-fourth president of the United States, Eisenhower was born on October 14, 1890, the third of seven children, in Texas. Before his election to the Oval Office in 1952, he served as the US Army Chief of Staff and was appointed to the position of Supreme Allied Commander

President Dwight D. Eisenhower gives a speech to the nation.

of NATO in 1951. He retired in 1961 and died in 1969. While most of his contributions to the space race took place during the time between the end of the Second World War and the launch of *Sputnik*, the opening moves of the Cold War (including the Korean War) paved the way for the concern felt by Americans. He initially wasn't concerned about Russia's space programs that were sending satellites into space first because he was more interested in "freedom of space." The idea was that space belonged to everyone, and satellites should be able to fly over foreign countries, allowing Americans to use surveillance satellites to identify Soviet missiles.

Many of Eisenhower's best-known contributions to history are from the Second World War, such as his involvement in the invasion of Normandy on June 6, 1944. This was one of the largest military invasions in history, during which Allied forces used many small boats to deliver soldiers to the beaches for the attack, which would help push German soldiers out of France. However, his early life is not without achievement. He was a football player in high school and college and joined the military after completing his schooling. While stationed in Texas, he met and married his wife, Mamie Geneva Doud. During the First World War, he trained soldiers at Gettysburg in the use of tanks.

John F. Kennedy

There are times when a voice for a nation becomes the will of a nation, times when the right speaker at the right time with the right words can inspire hundreds of thousands, even millions of people to act together for a common goal. Some of the best leaders in history are known for their speeches, and John F. Kennedy is one of them.

Before and during his time as thirty-fifth president of the United States, Kennedy advocated the importance of the United States's space program. At key points in the space race, Kennedy's voice was a rallying cry for America to continue despite hardships endured and dangers faced. His insistence on the importance of space exploration

President John F. Kennedy

and research is just one of the many reasons Kennedy is remembered in history books.

Born on May 17, 1917, Kennedy grew up in a family with wealth on both sides. He was the second child of nine siblings, many of whom also went on to achieve much during their lifetimes. Mischievous in his youth, Kennedy attended a Catholic boarding school and then a private preparatory school. Throughout his schooling, he excelled in courses he enjoyed and earned poor grades in courses that did not interest him. In high school, he continued to pursue his own interests at the cost of his grades. Mediocre performance in school combined with several illnesses that caused him to miss a great deal of his early education left his parents not expecting much from their son. It wouldn't be until his later years at Harvard University that he would show more seriousness with his studies, but his parents still didn't expect much from him.

Elected as president of the United States in 1961 after serving in the House of Representatives and then the Senate, Kennedy's optimism for the advancement of spaceflight technology and enthusiasm for the exploration and understanding of outer space helped turn the space race from a race for superiority over the Soviet Union into an effort the nation could be proud of for generations. He also set the clear finish line for the space race: the moon. But Kennedy's contributions to the space race are not all that he was known for. A historically popular president, Kennedy saw the rise of the Civil Rights Movement, dealt with the Cuban Missile Crisis in 1962, and had a hand in easing some nuclear tensions with the passing of the Nuclear Test Ban Act. Although his presidency and his life were cut short by his assassination in 1963, his efforts during his administration were still an important part of the space race.

John Glenn

As Alan Shepard had already proven before him, John Glenn was further evidence that slow and steady progress would win the space race. Although his orbit around Earth was not the first for humanity, it was the first for the United States. It was also further proof that the United States was making steady progress toward discovery and winning the space race.

Born in Cambridge, Ohio on July 18, 1921, John Glenn grew up in Ohio, attending high school and earning a bachelor of science from Muskingum College before taking

Astronaut John Glenn

part in the Second World War. As a Navy pilot, he flew fifty-nine combat missions on the Pacific front. He continued his service in the military through the Korean War before becoming a test pilot in 1957. During this time, he set the record for traveling from Los Angeles, California to New York City in just under three and a half hours.

On February 20, 1962, after being assigned as the back-up pilot for Mercury-Redstone missions 3 and 4, John Glenn made history by becoming the first American to orbit Earth. When he returned to Earth safely after four hours and fifty-five minutes, he was greeted as a hero, earning various awards including the NASA Distinguished Service Medal. However, Glenn's part in American history was far from over. After becoming friends with President Kennedy, he was convinced that continuing a career in public service was a good idea. His first few attempts at running for public office were not successful, however.

In 1974, Glenn was elected to the US Senate and attempted to become the Democratic presidential nominee in 1984. In 1998, he became the oldest person to fly in space, aboard the *Discovery* shuttle. Although he retired from the Senate, he remained a hero to the American people as a symbol of both pioneering spirit and dedication to the nation. Glenn died at the age of 95 on December 6, 2016.

Lyndon B. Johnson

There are times when a movement is forged in a passion of enthusiasm and then tempered in adversity. The assassination of John F. Kennedy was such a moment for the American people as well as for the space race. With the loss of such a popular proponent of advancing space research, the space race could have sputtered out then and there, but the nation was not completely without guidance. Shortly after Kennedy's death, Vice President Lyndon B. Johnson was sworn in to the presidency and was determined to honor Kennedy's goal of reaching the moon.

Best known for his time in politics, Johnson was born on August 27, 1908 in Texas, where he grew up. He graduated from what would later become the Texas State University in 1930. Although he briefly worked as a schoolteacher, he quickly moved into the realm of politics after his appointment to the position of legislative secretary of a Texas congressman. During the Second World War, Johnson briefly served in the US Navy Reserves but returned to Washington, DC, after his tour ended. He served as a senator for Texas in 1948 and was the leader for the Democrats, who held a minority in congress until 1953. Johnson also served as majority leader when the Democrats gained the majority in congress. He ran alongside John F. Kennedy for the presidential election of 1960, in which he became the vice president of the United States.

Although the most prominent speeches and enthusiasm for the space race came from President Kennedy, Johnson was in charge of overseeing the US space program and NASA. He endorsed the efforts of the president and NASA even after Kennedy's assassination. Where Kennedy rallied the nation's support and vigor, Johnson kept the effort alive by continuing to lead the nation as NASA worked toward the goal of winning the space race.

Margaret Hamilton

When remembering the space race, it's easiest to recall the names of the first astronauts to orbit Earth, the first to walk on the moon, and the presidents and other leaders of the time. But no less important are those who worked behind the scenes, contributing vital information and discoveries that made the flights of the astronauts a possibility at all. These people, who are sometimes left out of many history books until years after the fact, are the unsung heroes of the space race. One such person is Margaret Hamilton, the computer programmer who helped put the Apollo 11 boots on moon dust.

Born in 1936, Margaret Hamilton attended college in Michigan where she earned a bachelor degree in mathematics in 1958. Later, she graduated from Massachusetts Institute of Technology. According to NASA,

> With her colleagues, she developed the building blocks for modern 'software engineering,' a term Hamilton coined. What later became the foundations for her Universal Systems Language (001AXES) and Development Before the Fact (DBTF) formal systems theory, allowed the team to create what she called ultra-reliable software for the moon trip. In addition to creating the concept of priority displays, where the software in an emergency could interrupt the astronauts so they could reconfigure in realtime, Hamilton established hard requirements on the engineering of all components and subsystems, insisted on

debugging all component and testing everything before assembly, then simulated every conceivable situation at the systems level to identify potential problems before releasing the code.

Michael Collins

Even the one-man spaceflights made by Glenn and Shepard were not the product of their efforts alone. Every mission conducted by NASA was the product of the efforts of hundreds, even thousands of people, working together toward the common goal of making history and earning new knowledge. Although he did not walk on the moon alongside Neil Armstrong and Buzz Aldrin, Collins's skills as a pilot and his other contributions to the mission ensured its overall success.

Born on October 31, 1930 in Rome, Italy, where his father was stationed for the US military, Collins attended St. Albans School in Washington, DC, and West Point Military Academy in New York, where he graduated in 1952 with a bachelor of science degree. Soon after graduation, he joined the Air Force, where he showed himself to be a talented pilot. While his first application for an astronaut position was not accepted, he still joined the Aerospace Research Pilot School in the Air Force to gain more knowledge and experience regarding space and spaceflight. In 1963, he was chosen to be part of another group of astronauts.

Collins's time as an astronaut required him to participate in two spaceflights. The first was in 1966, where he performed a spacewalk, and the second was as part of the Apollo 11 mission that placed Buzz Aldrin and

Insights from the Astronauts

Sometimes it's easy to separate the acts of people in a history book from the fact that they were actual people with thoughts, feelings, and opinions of their own. This collection of quotes from astronauts and cosmonauts alike is here to show the genuine human side to these historic individuals.

Alan Shepard:

"It's a very sobering feeling to be up in space and realize that one's safety factor was determined by the lowest bidder on a government contract."

"They say any landing you can walk away from is a good one."

John Glenn:

"The most important thing we can do is inspire young minds and to advance the kind of science, math and technology education that will help youngsters take us to the next phase of space travel."

"Any administration foolish enough to call ketchup a vegetable cannot be expected to cut the mustard."

Buzz Aldrin:

"Whenever I gaze up at the moon, I feel like I'm on a time machine. I am back to that precious pinpoint of time, standing on the foreboding—yet beautiful—Sea of Tranquility.

I could see our shining blue planet Earth poised in the darkness of space."

"There's a historical milestone in the fact that our Apollo 11 landing on the moon took place a mere 66 years after the Wright Brothers' first flight."

Neil Armstrong:

"It suddenly struck me that that tiny pea, pretty and blue, was Earth. I put up my thumb and shut one eye, and my thumb blotted out the planet Earth. I didn't feel like a giant. I felt very, very small."

"It's a brilliant surface in that sunlight. The horizon seems quite close to you because the curvature is so much more pronounced than here on Earth. It's an interesting place to be. I recommend it."

Valentina Tereshkova:

"One cannot deny the great role women have played in the world community. My flight was yet another impetus to continue this female contribution."

"It doesn't matter what country or what political system you are from. Space brings you together."

Neil Armstrong on the moon's surface. Upon their safe return, President Richard Nixon awarded all three astronauts with the Presidential Medal of Freedom. Although Aldrin and Armstrong received most of the public awareness and attention, Collins's contributions were vital in returning the first moon walkers home safely.

Neil Armstrong

Born in Ohio on August 5, 1930, Neil Armstrong was very interested in airplanes, rockets, and flight from an early age. At the age of only sixteen, Armstrong had earned a student pilot's license, signaling the beginning of his long career as a pilot. In 1947, with the financial help of a US

Astronaut Neil Armstrong

Navy scholarship, Armstrong attended and graduated Purdue University and joined the Navy afterward. As a pilot in the navy, he fought in the Korean War, flying seventy-eight combat missions. In 1952, he left the military in favor of pursuing further education at Purdue University. Just a few short years later, Armstrong joined up with the NACA, which later became NASA.

After returning to Earth from the Apollo 11 mission, Armstrong continued to work with NASA until 1971 as the Deputy Associate Administrator for Aeronautics and would continue to be involved, although less directly, with the United States's space program. After the *Challenger* shuttle disaster of the 1980s, he served on the incident's presidential commission as vice chairman.

Although he gained a great deal of notoriety from the success of the Apollo 11 mission, Armstrong never seemed comfortable with the idea of being a celebrity, shying away from the public view in favor of his own privacy. However, he did participate in an interview for the *60 Minutes* news show in 2005. In 2010, when President Barack Obama announced the cancellation of several planned NASA missions, including one that would have taken people to the moon again, Armstrong spoke out against giving up the United States's role in exploration and research. Armstrong passed away in 2012 due to complications during heart surgery.

Nikita Khrushchev

An important fact to remember about the space race is that it was a part of the Cold War, a real struggle between two major civilizations that could determine the fate of the free world and perhaps humanity as a whole.

Nikita Sergeyevich Khrushchev was born on April 15, 1894, in Russia near the Ukrainian border. After a short time as a factory worker in his teen years, he joined the Red Army and fought in the Russian Revolution. Soon after, he gained an education, became a Communist, and quickly rose through the ranks of Soviet government. In 1953, after Stalin's death, Khrushchev became the leader of the Soviet Union's Communist Party. Although he spent a great deal of time denouncing the actions of Stalin, much to the shock of many of Stalin's supporters, he still used similar tactics as Stalin to maintain his position as party leader and prevent deposition after any of his decisions proved to be contested by other prominent party members.

Much of Khrushchev's political history paints him as erratic, appearing to be shrewd and tactical at times and belligerent and threatening at others. Depending on who his audience was, he could appear to have an entirely different temperament. He enjoyed verbal sparring matches with his opponents, including one famous one between himself and President Richard Nixon over kitchen appliances.

Wernher von Braun

Major points in history can often be defined by the minds that drove their progress. For World War I, it was the engineering feats of John Browning, Hiram Maxim, and

Richard Gatling. World War II brought the genius works of Albert Einstein to light. The Cold War and the space race, however, will always belong to Dr. Wernher von Braun.

Born on March 23, 1912, in what is now Wyrzysk, Poland, Wernher von Braun gained an interest in astronomy as a child, which became a growing desire to learn about space and interplanetary travel. After graduating from the Berlin Institute of Technology in 1932 with a bachelor's degree, he studied physics at the University of Berlin. In 1945, von Braun and his research team surrendered to American soldiers and signed a contract agreeing to work for the United States for a year. He later was put in charge of the US Army Ordinance Guided Missile Project, a position where his major responsibility was advancing the United States's rocket technologies, one of the most important aspects of both the space race and the arms race. Von Braun became a legal United States citizen, continuing to work throughout the space race. Starting with the launch of the *Explorer 1* satellite, aspects of von Braun's research and efforts would become part of every rocket launch thereafter.

Although he was good at his job, von Braun faced some poor treatment due to his history working for Germany in the Second World War. Still, over the course of his career as a rocket scientist, he earned the respect of many of his colleagues as well as many awards and honors from organizations in his field. Although much of his research was initially used for military purposes, his contributions to rocket science made several successful missions possible.

Fallen Stars

A somber part of any account of a time in history is the recording of deaths of those who took part in that era. This section is here to both make note of the deaths and honor the lives of important figures in the space race.

November 3, 1957
Laika passes away aboard *Sputnik 2*.

November 22, 1963
President John F. Kennedy is assassinated.

October 31, 1964
Astronaut Theodore Freeman dies when his T-38 jet crashes.

February 28, 1966
Astronauts Charles Bassett and Elliot See die in a plane crash.

January 27, 1967
Astronauts Gus Grissom, Ed White, and Roger Chaffee die in a fire inside the capsule of *Apollo 1*.

April 24, 1967
Cosmonaut Vladimir Komarov dies when his capsule impacts Earth after the parachute fails to open properly.

June 6, 1967

Astronaut Edward Givens dies in a car accident.

October 5, 1967

Astronaut Clifton Williams dies in a plane crash.

March 27, 1968

Cosmonaut Yuri Gagarin dies in a plane crash.

Although it is not easy or pleasant to remember history through the process of recounting deaths and tragedies, the death of an astronaut in the Cold War was regarded as a victory for the other side. But the death of an astronaut also showed that the effort to explore space was too dangerous with not enough reward. Although the field of space travel has always been one of the more dangerous areas of science, many of the surviving astronauts later went on to advocate for the importance of those same programs.

The logo for the National Aeronautics
and Space Administration (NASA)

CHAPTER FOUR

Negotiation and Innovation

The process that would become the birth of the National Aeronautics and Space Administration (NASA) was started by the launch of *Sputnik* in 1957. It was clear that something had to be done to prevent Soviet superiority in space technology, but it was unclear which government agency should be placed in charge of the American space program. The National Science Foundation (NSF), Atomic Energy Commission (AEC), National Advisory Committee for Aeronautics (NACA), US Army and US Air Force all would have gladly taken on the project and subsequent boost in funding, but there were still concerns with any of these choices. According to an article on NASA's website,

> *If it was [a] military or civilian agency, then how to divide the tasks peculiar to each function? Should the new agency include aeronautical activities? Should it have the power to*

implement international agreements, how should
those agreements be used as an instrument of
foreign policy, and what should the new agency's
relationship be with the State Department?

The Foundation of NASA

At first, it seemed as if the NACA would be the agency placed in charge of the space program for the nation, but rather than strengthen the NACA, President Eisenhower drafted the initial legislation to create the National Aeronautics and Space Administration, an entirely new agency that was not based in the military but would cooperate with military scientists and offer any new information of military value. In total, NASA's directives were the following: to learn about space, to improve rocket technology, to create space vehicles capable of carrying both equipment and living passengers, to understand what might be gained from peaceful space studies, to make and keep the United States a leader in space technology, to give any discoveries of military importance to the military, to cooperate with other nations toward peaceful space research, and to cooperate with other government agencies to make sure no two agencies wasted funding doing the same research.

Over the years, the legislation surrounding the formation of NASA would be edited and fine-tuned as needed, but its position as the government agency in charge of winning the space race, of promoting discovery and exploration of space, and of spearheading new space-age technologies was cemented in history. Today, NASA is still in charge of space research and still conducts missions to gather information about our solar system and the space beyond.

Rockets

Prior to the onset of the space race, the main use for rocket technology was to launch destructive payloads for military purposes. Toward the end of the Second World War, Germany had scientists working on rockets for this very reason, with more than three thousand rockets fired at Allied targets before the war's end. Their speed, long range, and impressive destructive capability made the previous standard of using several large planes to carry large numbers of inaccurate bombs to drop on targets in a practice called "carpet bombing." Bomber missions were, in comparison to rockets, very slow and very risky in terms of personnel and resource requirements. They were also vulnerable because even the most advanced bombers in the US military were easy targets for fighter pilots, especially with the implementation of early jet aircraft toward the end of the war. This meant that any bombing mission needed to be carried out in large numbers, with a significant number of fighter planes escorting the bombers to protect them from enemy planes. The elimination of the need to risk so many troops to carry out such missions was of great strategic importance, then, especially with the creation of atomic weaponry.

The race to create more advanced rockets in higher quantities became a major part of both the space race and the Cold War. An arms race was in full swing while NASA

One of the many rockets that NASA launched as part of its research

attempted to find ways to safely use the same technology the military was using for war to deliver scientific equipment and eventually put people into space.

One of the biggest developments in rocket technology was the separation of rockets into multiple sections, or stages, which would each expend their fuel in order to deliver something to space before disconnecting from the unspent parts of the rocket. This meant that different stages could use different fuels. The stages could also be calibrated to different compositions of Earth's atmosphere or become more maneuverable after the excess mass of the spent parts of the rocket were ejected. This multistage technology would also make it possible for satellites and capsules to be ejected from the spent rocket parts, leaving them unhindered by extra mass. Later rocket configurations would include parallel staging, where multiple rockets of different sizes were connected together, with smaller rockets providing the initial boost needed to get the rocket moving upward fast enough before separation, when the larger rocket could get the rest of the launch done alone.

At the same time that NASA was developing rockets to carry measuring devices and eventually people, the military was working on similar technology for military purposes. This period of development set the foundations for missile technologies that are still used by military forces today, such as missile guidance technology and improvements in missile detection and interception technology. At the time, most of this technology was used to make weapons like the intercontinental ballistic missile (ICBM), which was designed to carry nuclear payloads over great distances.

Two solid rocket boosters (SRBs) separate from the larger secondary rocket.

However, with the existence of radar technology (and eventually the use of surveillance satellites), either side of the Cold War was capable of detecting a nuclear launch with enough time to respond. This resulted in the strategy of mutually assured destruction (MAD) that both sides of the Cold War agreed upon.

Satellites

Early satellite technology was somewhat simple by today's standards. *Sputnik* held little more than a battery, a radio, and a thermometer when it was launched into orbit. Similarly, the *Explorer 1* satellite was equipped with a measuring instrument, a power source, and a radio to transmit information back to Earth; however, *Explorer 1* was made to measure radiation rather than temperature. In 1960, the *Echo 1* satellite was essentially a reflective metal balloon used to bounce transmissions from one spot on Earth to another, allowing communication over great distances. Commercial communication satellites were in use by the end of the decade and are still used today, but newer models with more advanced technology and solar panels for power generation are the standard.

The next major development in satellite technology was the addition of cameras, with Soviet satellites taking photos of the surface of the moon, and the *TIROS 1* satellite taking thousands of photographs of clouds and weather patterns on Earth's surface during its time in space. Cameras in satellites are still used to measure and predict weather patterns today, and at the time of their invention, it was a major breakthrough in the field of meteorology. In 1962, the launch of the *Telstar* satellite made transmissions of television signals across the Atlantic Ocean a possibility, allowing telecommunication on a scale never seen before. It was another step toward global communications, a technology we take for granted today.

Space Vehicles

Once scientists figured out that it was possible to carry larger and larger satellites as newer and better rocket technology emerged, it wasn't long before manned satellites, or space

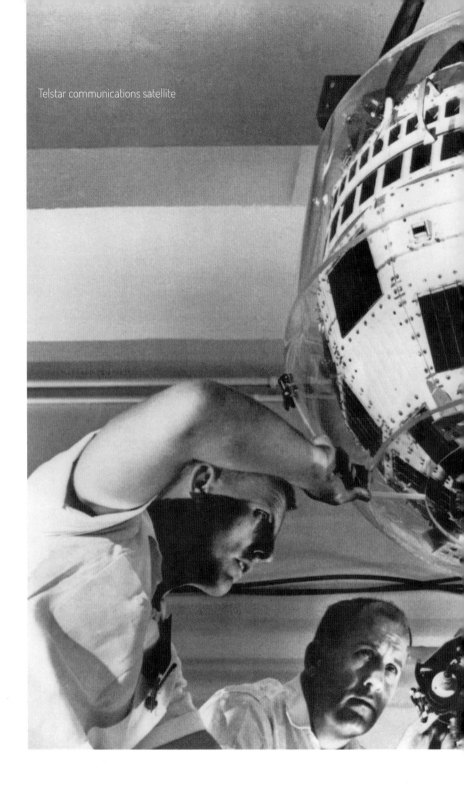

Telstar communications satellite

Sputnik and the Space Race

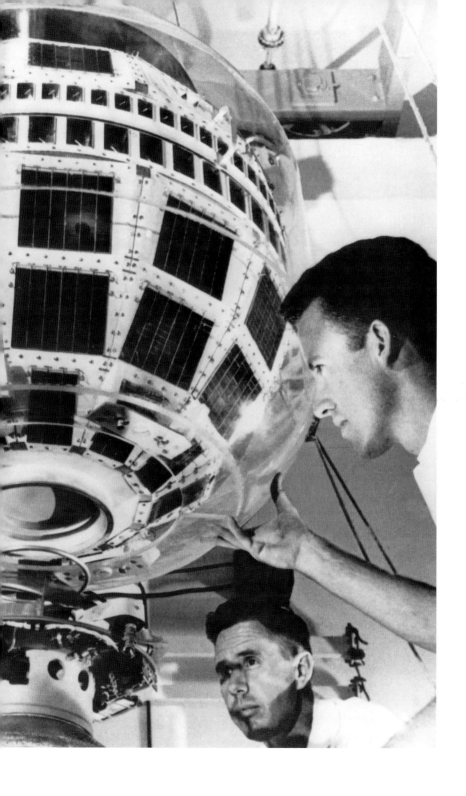

vehicles capable of safely carrying human passengers, were the next item to be developed. Although the Soviet space program's *Sputnik 2* carried a living passenger, Laika the dog, the technology needed to bring a passenger back safely was still years away. The biggest problem facing space vehicles is reentry. When the air resistance against an object is falling faster and faster due to gravity, an area of air compression is created that becomes very hot and threatens to damage or destroy whatever object is reentering.

Both sides of the space race worked on solving the issue of reentry in different ways. Yuri Gagarin's flight in 1961 used a capsule that implemented rockets to try to slow down the capsule's descent until he was close enough to landing that he could be ejected from the craft and parachute down. Later capsule models, such as the *Friendship 7* that carried John Glenn, had a heat shield that helped dissipate the intense heat from air compression as well as parachutes that helped the craft land safely. This combination of heat shields and parachutes would be the standard until the implementation of shuttles starting in 1972, which used heat shields but were able to land on earth like modern airplanes.

Computers

Rocket and satellite technology were not the only areas to experience a "boom" in advancement during the space race. Computers themselves experienced a boost in development in terms of power and capability. Up until the late 1940s, computers often filled entire rooms due to the need for bulky vacuum tubes. Then, with the invention of the transistor in

Data Storage

One of the biggest issues facing the development of computer technology was the ability to store information. If a computer couldn't store information, it was little better than an oversized calculator, after all.

Over the years, different ways to store information were developed with each new kind of computer. In the 1930s, magnetic drums emerged, but these storage devices didn't hold much data. In the 1940s, cathode ray tube devices could store 1024 bytes (one kilobyte) of information. The invention of the hard disk drive in the 1950s boosted the amount of data that could be stored to almost four megabytes. Each megabyte contained 1024 kilobytes. Larger units in the early 1960s could store just over two hundred megabytes.

Transporting data was still difficult because lightweight and portable storage wouldn't come about until the early 1970s, with the invention of the 8-inch floppy disk, which could hold just over one megabyte at most. One megabyte is enough to store just over a minute of an .mp3 recording or a few photographs or documents.

Today's storage media far surpasses anything available during the space race. Small devices are currently capable of holding more information than several filing cabinets filled up with paper. Medium-sized storage devices are capable of holding more than an entire library. The technology behind data storage is always getting smaller and cheaper over time as well, with the price per gigabyte of data dropping from hundreds of thousands of dollars in the 1980s to just a few cents today.

1947, computers had the ability to be made much smaller than before. In 1958, the invention of the integrated circuit, also known as a "computer chip," made it possible for computers to become even smaller and more powerful. Still, the computers used to conduct the Apollo 11 missions had less processing power than the average pocket calculator today, and modern mobile devices have capabilities far beyond what scientists could have dreamed of at that time. The advancements made in the two decades between the invention of the transistor and the first moon landing are no small feat.

Space Suits and Life Support

With the data gathered by satellites about the composition of Earth's upper atmosphere and the space beyond, scientists on both sides of the space race had another problem to contend with: How would they protect astronauts and other living passengers from the harmful cosmic rays, the lack of oxygen, and the oppressive vacuum of empty space? What would astronauts eat or drink?

Most of these problems could be solved with the proper engineering of space vehicles to carry supplies of oxygen. These vehicles could also have the structural integrity to withstand the pressures and stresses of the launch and orbit; however, other issues such as food and hydration created new problems and concerns. Water was stored in lightweight plastic containers, but food had to be modified to make it more efficient for space travel. At first, it wasn't certain that being in low gravity or **zero gravity** would interfere with the ability to chew, swallow, or digest food. However, once

Astronaut Eugene Cernan tests the Lunar Roving Vehicle (LRV) on the surface of the moon.

Bathrooms in Space

What is an astronaut to do when the nearest bathroom is hundreds of thousands of miles away on the surface of the earth? It isn't feasible to make return trips for every bathroom break, and the lack of gravity poses an entirely different obstacle to normal waste removal. Removing waste is a crucial biological function for people on land or in space, and the problem of figuring out how to handle the issue of needing a bathroom in space was a definite concern.

Early solutions for single-person spacecraft included simple urinal devices hooked up to tubes that would collect and store urine, but solid waste was a whole different issue. According to Mark Roberts, in the article "The Scoop on Space Poop: How Astronauts Go Potty," "'Whatever comes out of you doesn't know it's supposed to come away from you.'" The article further explains, "Each fecal collection bag came with a 'finger cot' to allow the astronauts to manually move things along. Then they had to knead a germicide into their waste so that gas-expelling bacteria wouldn't flourish inside the sealed bag and cause it to explode."

Eventually, systems involving toilet-like devices that use vacuum pressure to collect, store, and eject both solid and liquid waste from the spacecraft were created. While these space toilets are slightly easier to use, the technique for properly using the bathroom in space requires special training because the mechanisms involved could become clogged and cause a messy problem for astronauts. Today, filtration systems capable of turning urine into water safe for drinking are aboard the international space station.

it was shown not to interfere with any of those processes, the main issue with food rations in space was their weight, as every ounce of cargo had to be accounted for in a rocket launch. The first astronaut food rations were stored in metal tubes similar to toothpaste, but the process of freeze-drying and vacuum-sealing food made rations lighter and tastier for astronauts while also preserving them so there was no need for refrigeration. These rations could be eaten in their freeze-dried state or injected with hot water to heat and hydrate them for the astronauts' consumption. Freeze-dried ice cream and other space-faring foods are still available for purchase today.

As for travel outside of a spacecraft, space suits were equipped with multiple layers of tough insulation to withstand the extreme variations in temperature that could occur in space. They also had air-conditioning systems to help regulate the internal temperatures of the suits. Spacesuits were also equipped with their own supplies of oxygen, emergency liquid nutrition and water supplies, and communication equipment. These technologies allowed for spacewalks and served as a contingency in case the capsule lost pressure, making it unsafe to be outside a suit inside the craft. The entire suit with life support systems weighed a few hundred pounds, but with the reduced gravity of orbit and the moon, the weight was less of an issue.

A shuttle midflight with
its large doors open

CHAPTER FIVE

The Legacy of the Space Race

Although the space race had reached a peaceful conclusion, with both sides growing to view each other as friendly rivals, the Cold War was still going on at the same time. The Soviet Union was still a major contender in the arms race, but while the United States and the Soviet Union were locked in their rivalry to race to the moon, other events around the world continued to make the Cold War a tense and ever-changing concern.

Cuba

In 1959, Fidel Castro became the new leader of Cuba and installed a Communist government. In 1961, after a failed invasion attempt by Cuban refugees trained by the United States, Castro's place in power was shown to be quite secure. The Bay of Pigs Invasion, as it was called, surrendered to Castro's overwhelming forces after just one day of fighting. In 1962, the situation with Cuba became infinitely more tense when the Soviet Union cooperated with Cuba to install nuclear weapons in its territory. These missiles, less than a hundred miles from American shores, would be capable of delivering a nuclear payload almost anywhere in the United States. The period of tense negotiation surrounding this event was known as the Cuban Missile Crisis. President John F. Kennedy informed the public that he was prepared to use military action if necessary, but the tension was resolved when Kennedy and Russian leader Nikita Khrushchev reached an agreement. The Soviet Union would withdraw its weapons from Cuba, and Kennedy would withdraw some

The destruction of the Berlin Wall was a symbolic moment, signaling the beginning of the end of the Cold War.

American weapons from Turkey in exchange. An embargo against Cuba, which prohibited travel to and trade with Cuba, was placed into effect in 1960 when Castro took power. In 2009, the travel restrictions were relaxed somewhat, and diplomatic and trade relations with Cuba today appear to be moving toward an ending of the embargo.

The Berlin Wall

By 1961, Berlin had largely split into Communist-led East Berlin and capitalist West Berlin. The government of East Berlin built a wall made out of concrete and barbed wire that split the city in an attempt to prevent what they believed to be undermining influences of capitalism. The divide between East and West Berlin remained until 1989, when the boundary was dissolved and the wall was torn down.

The Vietnam War

Lasting ten years, the Vietnam War was a long and bloody conflict that took place between Communist-led forces in North Vietnam and its allies, and South Vietnam, whose primary alliance was with the United States. The Vietnam War is notorious for being one of the bloodiest and most brutal conflicts in United States history, due to its guerrilla-style warfare and difficult fighting conditions. As the war went on, it became less and less popular with the American people for several reasons. First, there was a military draft, which could select young men of military age into training so they could be implemented in the conflict. Second, there was a growing rift between what the American government told its people about the progress of the war and what was actually occurring overseas. Third, with the growing ability of American news media to cover the war (due in part to the use of telecommunications satellites launched during the space race), the American people were exposed to the horrific civilian casualties that came as a result of the war, leading to protests all over the nation—including one protest at Kent State University in Ohio that led to the shooting of civilian protesters by US National Guard troops in 1970. The Vietnam War ended with the fall of South Vietnam to Communist forces in 1975.

China

In 1949, a civil war in China ended when Communist forces claimed victory. Because of this, the United States cut off diplomatic ties with China. This lack of contact grew more tense as China allied with the Communist forces of North Korea during the Korean War, and worries about China grew again during the Vietnam War. In 1964, when China detonated its first atomic bomb, it appeared that China was about to enter the Cold War as another major player on the side of Communism. However, as relations between the Soviet Union and the United States were becoming less tense over the course of the space race, politicians in China and the Soviet Union began to disagree on how they should treat the United States, and the disagreement grew to violence in 1971 during the Sino-Soviet border conflict. The fighting ended quickly, but relations between the Soviet Union and

China would remain poor until the end of the Cold War. That same year, President Richard Nixon visited China, beginning the process of reestablishing diplomatic relations.

Ending the Cold War

One of the biggest turning points that marked the beginning of the end of the Cold War was the rise to power of Mikhail Gorbachev, who became the leader of the Soviet Union in 1985. In 1989, the fall of the Berlin Wall became a symbol many hoped would mean the reunification of Germany, a process that was hinted at earlier that year when East Germany started to allow people to leave and migrate to West Germany. In 1990, Gorbachev and President George Bush successfully negotiated the reunification of Germany once and for all. Due to Gorbachev's loosening of the Soviet Union's hold on other nations, it seemed as if the Soviet Union would soon cease to be, as various nations under its rule became independent and democratic. After an unsuccessful coup attempt by communists seeking to reclaim Soviet control, the Soviet Union was abolished, and Boris Yeltsin became the president of Russia, signaling the end of the Cold War in 1991.

Life After the Moon Walkers: The End of the Apollo Program

After the American victory in the space race with the Apollo 11 mission, and the cultural impact created by the opportunity to view Earth as a planet and not a mere collection of nations, the call for humans to continue to explore, discover, and innovate in the fields of space exploration and space travel continues to drive NASA and its counterparts throughout the world. Many of the technologies that were invented or used out of necessity during the space race have become ubiquitous, such as satellite television, Velcro, and smoke detectors. Other tools that were used to allow people to walk on the moon have become more powerful as time and technology have progressed, such as personal computers and phones. However, the end of the space race prompted not only a shift toward exploring the rest of the solar system, but also toward using the same technologies to better understand Earth.

NASA continued to send people to space after Apollo 11, with Apollo missions 13, 14, and 16 in 1970, 1971, and 1972 respectively. The last manned moon landing was the Apollo 17 mission in December of 1972. In 1975, the Apollo-Soyuz project paved the way for international cooperation in space travel and exploration. This project was also the last in the Apollo series of missions, which totaled six moon landings and many hours of time in space for astronauts.

The Challenger Disaster

In 1986, a mission to carry a space shuttle crewed by a collection of American citizens with various backgrounds in terms of race, religion, gender, and geography was scheduled to be launched on the morning of January 28, from the Kennedy Space Center in Florida. Disaster struck when a leak in one of the smaller solid rocket boosters caused the

The crew of the Challenger mission

larger liquid-fueled rocket to ignite, exploding and killing all
seven of the Challenger's crew, Francis R. Scobee, Michael
J. Smith, Judith A. Resnik, Ronald E. McNair, Ellison S.
Onizuka, Gregory B. Jarvis, and Christa McAuliffe. The
launch, which was being broadcast around the globe, shocked
and saddened many, and future launches were put on hold

Hubble Telescope and its Successors

In 1990, the Hubble space telescope was launched. The project, which had been in development since the 1970s, nearly ended in failure due to a near-microscopic flaw in a mirror in the telescope's inner workings. However, with the aid of computers and a repair mission in 1993,

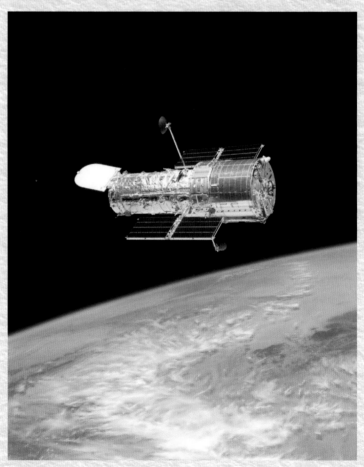

The Hubble space telescope in orbit

the Hubble space telescope has provided important images of objects both inside and outside of our solar system. It continues to operate to this day, providing images of space through both the visual and ultraviolet spectrums of light.

The next space telescope to join Hubble as a means to observe space was the Chandra telescope, an extremely powerful x-ray telescope with the ability to observe and measure the x-rays emitted by extremely hot objects within its range. According to Space.com, "It has found previously hidden black holes, provided observations of the Milky Way's own supermassive black hole, Sagittarius A*, and even taken the first x-ray images of Mars."

The Spitzer space telescope, the last of Hubble's counterparts, was launched in 2003, with the goal of taking images of space in the infrared section of the spectrum of light. While Hubble already had some infrared capability, Spitzer had the advantage of range. Spitzer is nearing the end of its projected lifespan, which relies on a supply of coolant that is soon to expire. Its planned successor, the Herschel telescope, was launched in 2009. With the Planck Observatory, it uses microwaves to observe some of the last bits of stray light from massive cosmic events while attempting to gain more information on "dark matter."

until the cause of the explosion could be properly investigated and preventive measures could be implemented. This also delayed plans that were in progress to build and launch an international space station.

Space Stations: An International Cooperation for the Future

One of the next and biggest steps for both NASA's and Russia's space program was the establishment of manned, orbiting space stations. The first space station came in the form of the United States's Skylab, which orbited Earth from 1973 to 1979. Its purpose was to act as an observatory as well as a laboratory for a long list of experiments, ranging from testing the effects of cosmic radiation on different materials to measuring the long-term effects of zero-gravity on astronauts. Eventually, experiments aboard the Skylab space station concluded. The last crew members to leave and return to Earth left a few supplies, and they left the main hatch unlocked in case any other astronauts wanted to visit the craft. Its orbit eventually decayed, and it reentered Earth's atmosphere in 1979, splashing down in the ocean a few hundred miles off the coast of Australia.

The next major space station was the Mir space station, which lasted from 1986 to 2001. This is much longer than was initially expected. "Mir" means "peace" in Russian, and it represented a major step toward the peace sought by both sides of the Cold War, which ended during its service as a space station. It too was to serve as an environment for experiments in space. It held various facilities including one that was used to grow plants from seed. Over the years of its service, new modules and parts were added in cooperative efforts between the United States and Russia, and by the end of its fifteen-year service, several records for long-term space residence were set by its crew. It reentered orbit in 2001 and broke up and splashed into the ocean.

The most current space station is the International Space Station (ISS). The project for the ISS started in 1984, and the first part of the space station was launched into orbit in 1998, followed by a few more modules launched by the United States between 1998 and 2005. In 2008, two modules, one made by a European cooperative and one from Japan, were launched and joined the ISS, which still orbits Earth today. Like its predecessors, it is used by its crew to conduct experiments in the fields of physics, chemistry, and biology. It also serves as an international education opportunity for students around the world who wrote emails and asked questions of the crew members residing on the ISS. Those members responded with video transmissions, demonstrating things like what happens when a wet cloth is wrung out in zero gravity (zero-g) conditions.

The Importance of Continuing Exploration

While the pace of NASA and its counterparts' missions around the globe have not stopped, NASA has ceased to plan any further missions to the moon, focusing instead on unmanned missions that use satellites, probes, and rovers to explore the moon, Mars, and other planets in our solar

Astronauts float in zero gravity aboard the International Space Station (ISS).

system. In the last few years, in fact, two notable missions included a very successful landing of a rover capable of conducting tests on dirt and rocks onto the surface of Mars, and a satellite mission that flew past the dwarf planet of Pluto, providing some of the most detailed images of the surface of Earth's most distant neighbor in the solar system. As in the space race, whenever a major mission to send something to a faraway world becomes a unifying goal for NASA and American industries, human ingenuity and innovation prove time and time again that humanity is capable of reaching further, learning more, and discovering greater things than before. Yet, NASA now only accounts for a very small portion of the multibillion-dollar industry that is space exploration.

During the space race, and the decade after, space exploration represented the newest and brightest frontier for humanity. It was a shining opportunity for people, businesses, and governments to come together and achieve what was previously considered impossible. The national fervor created by the space race encouraged students to study in the fields of science and mathematics, as these subjects were what put people on the moon. Now, NASA seems to have become less of a priority, as its budget has shrunk sharply since the height of the space race. Every setback faced by NASA threatens to snuff out the thirst for exploration that the space race fostered, despite its initial birth in the fear of Communism.

One little satellite, a ball of metal containing a radio, a battery, and a thermometer set in motion a series of events that culminated with human beings standing on another world. It also encouraged the cooperation of humans, who carried machinery and equipment capable of housing them among the stars. It gave rise to the belief that one day human beings could travel to new worlds and have an opportunity to learn from our mistakes. It started a movement that showed just how amazing human beings can be, despite our many flaws. It set forth a boom in technology, industry, diplomacy, and curiosity. It opened our eyes to the fact that our blue planet is so very small and to the fact that there is so much left in the galaxy, in the universe, to explore. There's lots of room in future history books for more astronauts, and if the urge to explore and discover still exists in future generations, then it might still be possible for humanity to take a cue from science fiction and boldly go where none have gone before.

Chronology

1945   World War II ends. Potsdam Conference takes place.

1948   The Berlin Airlift starts.

1949   NATO is founded. Soviet Union explodes its first atomic weapon. Berlin Airlift ends.

1950   Korean War begins.

1953   US-assisted coup in Iran, Korean War ends.

1954   SEATO is founded.

1955   Warsaw Pact is founded. Geneva Summit takes place.

1957   The USSR launches *Sputnik 1* and *Sputnik 2*.

1958   The United States launches *Explorer 1* and *Vanguard 1*. The USSR launches *Sputnik 3*. NASA is founded.

1959   The USSR launches *Luna 1*, *Luna 2*, and *Luna 3*.

1960   The United States launches *Tiros 1* and *Discoverer XIV*. John F. Kennedy becomes thirty-fifth president of the United States.

1961	Yuri Gagarin of the USSR is the first man in space. Alan Shepard becomes the first American in space. Gherman Titov of the USSR spends a day in orbit.
1962	Americans John Glenn and Walter Schirra orbit Earth.
1963	L. Gordon Cooper of the United States spends thirty-four hours in space. Valentina Terashkova of the USSR becomes the first woman in space. John F. Kennedy is assassinated.
1964	*Ranger 7* takes pictures of the moon.
1965	Alexei Leonov of the USSR makes the first spacewalk. Ed White becomes the first American to walk in space. The United States sends *Gemini 7*, which begins orbit.
1966	The USSR's *Luna 9* and the United States' *Surveyor 1* make soft landings on the moon. The USSR's *Luna 10* and the United States' *Lunar Orbiter 1* orbit the moon.
1967	The United States' *Apollo 1* accident occurs. The USSR's *Soyuz 1* accident occurs.
1968	The USSR's *Zond 5* passes by the moon and returns to Earth. *Apollo 8* orbits the moon.
1969	The USSR's Soyuz 4 and 5 rendezvous in orbit. The United States' Apollo 11 lands on the moon.

Glossary

astronaut A person who travels in space, either as a pilot or a passenger.

Berlin Airlift The effort to deliver supplies of food and water to those trapped in Berlin during the Cold War.

Berlin Wall A concrete border built by Communist-led East Berlin to separate it from East Berlin.

capitalism An economic system in which businesses are not all controlled by the government.

Cold War The period of tension between the United States and USSR between 1947 and 1991.

Communism An economic system in which all property is publicly owned.

cosmonaut A Russian astronaut.

missile A projectile weapon.

mutually assured destruction (MAD) The doctrine of military strategy in which the use of nuclear weapons would cause annihilation of both the attacker and its enemy.

NASA The National Aeronautics and Space Administration is an agency that serves the United States federal government and is responsible for space programs and research.

NATO The North Atlantic Treaty Organization is an alliance of countries from North America and Europe that was formed after the signing of a treaty on April 4, 1949.

orbit The path of an object affected by gravity that does not immediately return to its starting point.

rocket A projectile that can be used as either a missile or a vehicle.

satellite Any object that orbits a planet, usually refers to spacecraft in orbit.

SEATO The Southeast Asia Treaty Organization was formed in order to prevent Communism from spreading.

space The area beyond Earth's atmosphere.

spacewalk Any time spent by an astronaut outside of their spacecraft.

Sputnik The first artificial satellite to orbit Earth.

USSR The Union of Soviet Socialist Republics, also known as the Soviet Union, was governed by the Communist Party.

zero gravity (zero-g) Any environment where gravity seems to be absent.

Bibliography

Dunbar, Brian. "Biography: John Glenn." NASA, July 31, 2015. https://www.nasa.gov/centers/glenn/about/bios/glennbio.html.

"Edgar Faure." Encyclopedia Britannica Online. Accessed November 04, 2016. https://www.britannica.com/biography/Edgar-Jean-Faure.

"Eisenhower Presents His 'Open Skies' Plan." History.com. Accessed November 04, 2016. http://www.history.com/this-day-in-history/eisenhower-presents-his-open-skies-plan.

"Explorer 1 Overview." NASA, July 30, 2015. https://www.nasa.gov/mission_pages/explorer/explorer-overview.html.

"Korean War." History.com. Accessed November 04, 2016. http://www.history.com/topics/korean-war.

"Launch of First Crewed Gemini Flight." NASA, March 23, 2015. http://www.nasa.gov/content/march-23-1965-launch-of-first-crewed-gemini-flight/.

"Mariner 2: First Spacecraft to Another Planet." Space.com, December 3, 2012. http://www.space.com/18746-mariner-2.html.

"Milestones: 1937–1945." US Department of State. Accessed November 04, 2016. https://history.state. gov/milestones/1937-1945/potsdam-conf.

"The Sad Story of Laika, the First Dog Launched into Orbit." *Time*, November 03, 2015. http://time. com/3546215/laika-1957/.

"Spacecraft Details: Sputnik 3." NASA. Accessed November 04, 2016. http://nssdc.gsfc.nasa.gov/nmc/ spacecraftDisplay.do?id=1958-004B.

"Sputnik Launched." History.com. Accessed November 04, 2016. http://www.history.com/this-day-in-history/ sputnik-launched.

"Truman Doctrine is Announced." History.com. Accessed November 04, 2016. http://www.history. com/this-day-in-history/truman-doctrine-is-announced.

"The Warsaw Pact Is Formed." History.com. Accessed November 04, 2016. http://www.history.com/this-day-in-history/the-warsaw-pact-is-formed.

Further Information

Books

Cadbury, Deborah. *Space Race: The Epic Battle Between America and the Soviet Union for Dominion of Space.* New York: Harper Perennial, 2007.

Grove, Tim. *First Flight Around the World: The Adventures of the American Fliers Who Won the Space Race.* New York: Harry N. Abrams, 2015.

Scott, David, and Alexei Leonov. *Two Sides of the Moon: Our Story of the Cold War Space Race.* New York: St. Martin's Griffin, 2006.

Shetterly, Margot Lee. *Hidden Figures: The American Dream and the Untold Story of the Black Women Mathematicians Who Helped Win the Space Race.* New York: William Morrow, 2016.

Websites

Biography.com

http://www.biography.com

This site contains articles focusing on specific people from history, including information on their early life, education, families, achievements, and legacies.

History.com

http://www.history.com

History.com offers a collection of articles about the history of America and the rest of the world, and the website is associated with the History Channel on television.

NASA Website

http://www.nasa.gov

The official website of the National Aeronautics and Space Administration features articles about missions conducted by NASA from the space race to missions underway today.

TheSpaceRace.com

http://www.thespacerace.com

A website for students and enthusiasts alike, this site contains more information on the space race, including short biographies on many astronauts.

Videos

The Space Race

http://www.history.com/topics/space-race

This video accompanies an article that gives an overview of the battle for technological dominance during the space race.

**USA vs. USSR Fight! The Cold War:
Crash Course World History #39**

https://www.youtube.com/watch?v=y9HjvHZfCUI

This episode from an educational series teaches about the Cold War using animations and easy-to-follow language.

We Stopped Dreaming (Episode 1)

https://www.youtube.com/watch?v=CbIZU8cQWXc

This video, made by an advocate of space, features speeches given by famous scientist Neil deGrasse Tyson and contains footage from different space missions.

Index

Page numbers in **boldface** are illustrations, Entries in **boldface** are glossary terms,

About the Author

Jordan Johnson is a blind writer and science-fiction geek from Wisconsin. He has met Homer Hickam and two other people from NASA, gone to space camp, and his third-grade teacher once shook hands with Buzz Aldrin. Together with his wife, he travels the Midwest in search of the perfect hand-made soap and makes four-legged friends whenever at all possible. He also visits family from time to time.